praying YOUR WAY THROUGH IVF

Stephanie Jeffreys

Praying your way through IVF
Copyright © 2019 by Stephanie Jeffreys
PUBLISHED BY: Renewed Perspective Coaching, LLC
ISBN-13: 978-1-7330607-0-7

All rights reserved. Printed in the United States of America. No part of this book may be used or reproduced in any manner whatsoever without written permission except in the case of brief quotations embodied in critical articles or reviews.

Scripture quotations marked (NIV) are taken from the Holy Bible, New International Version®, NIV®. Copyright © 1973, 1978, 1984, 2011 by Biblica, Inc.™ Used by permission of Zondervan. All rights reserved worldwide. www.zondervan.com The "NIV" and "New International Version" are trademarks registered in the United States Patent and Trademark Office by Biblica, Inc.™

Cover & Interior Design: Olivia Heyward

Dedication

This book is dedicated to the amazing, beautiful, strong and courageous women who have been told that In Vitro Fertilization (IVF) is a way to start or add to your family. This news may have taken your world by storm, but please know that you are not alone. In the pages of this book of prayers, may you find the strength you need to remain full of Hope, Faith, and Love.

Table of Contents

Introduction		1
My Prayer For You		4
Chapter One	For This Child I prayed	5
Chapter Two	Before you were formed in the womb	19
Chapter Three	With God all things are possible	33
Chapter Four	Lean not on your own understanding	47
Chapter Five	For I know the plans I have for you	61
Chapter Six	God will heal the broken hearted	77
Chapter Seven	Pray without Ceasing	91

INTRODUCTION

IVF is a journey that if given a choice no couple would want to take. From our first to last appointment my husband and I navigated our infertility journey in the most loving, compassionate, and supportive manner. My husband, often riding the emotional rollercoaster as a silent supportive passenger, nurturer, and encourager was present in every way I needed him to be. For the purpose of this book I will be primarily focusing on our IVF from my perspective.

IVF was a topic I knew very little about at first. I had personally never known anyone who went through IVF. I felt lost and I turned to social media, specifically Facebook. I joined a group called IVF Support. It was important for me to feel supported, to have a safe space to ask questions without feeling judged, because at that time, I felt like a failure as a woman.

Every morning I would log onto Facebook to see how my journey compared to other women's journeys. Some of the stories in the group, such as the woman who got pregnant on her first or second IVF attempt, gave me so much hope. While, other stories such as women on their fifth, sixth, or seventh attempt with no pregnancy, or the woman who had a miscarriage after hearing her child's heartbeat, broke my heart into a million pieces.

I distinctly remember one morning not knowing what to say to comfort these beautiful women who were all experiencing different ranges of emotions at the same time. Immediately I began praying, and halfway through the prayer for some reason I began to type them in the notebook on my phone. The thoughts that came to my mind were meant to go straight from my heart to the heart of God. God prompted me to post a prayer in the Facebook IVF Support group. It was my heart's desire to remind myself and other women that regardless of our infertility struggles, God loves us, and He has not forgotten us. For women to understand that infertility is not a form of punishment from God because of something we did, or did not do, in the past.

During my journey through IVF, prayer was the glue that held me together mentally, emotionally, and spiritually. Each chapter in this book describes a different phase of my IVF journey followed by five prayers. The prayers that I am sharing in this book were prayers that I wrote and prayed when I was in a very low place and needed to be reminded of God's unwavering love for me. My prayers reminded me of His promise that He knows that the plans that he has for me.

Every day I challenged myself to find three things to be grateful for. Writing three things that I was grateful for helped me notice the small things that I would usually take for granted. Reflecting on the prayers after they were written helped me to understand where I was emotionally.

INTRODUCTION

On the days when I felt as though I was on an emotional rollercoaster I would journal until I felt the rollercoaster come to a complete stop.

At the end of each prayer there is a space for you to share what you are grateful for and to reflect on the prayer. This is your safe place to be vulnerable, transparent, and honest about how your infertility journey is impacting you and a place where you allow your emotions to run free.

My Prayer For You

Heavenly And Gracious Father,

    As humbly as I know how, I come into your presence, with boldness asking you to cover this beautiful woman on her journey to motherhood. I don't know her story which led her to IVF, but I do know this is a process that can be mentally, emotionally, physically, financially, and spiritually challenging. I ask that you cover her and her family with your grace and mercy. Every morning Lord, meet them at the point of their needs. You also know the desires of her heart for motherhood, so I ask that you allow her desires to be manifested. Allow prayer to be a secret resting place amid any uncertainty. I pray that you cover her in the safety of your arms as you lead and guide her on this journey. Give her wisdom in her decision making, and more than anything give her peace of mind. May she and her family feel your presence every step of the way. These and other blessings I ask in your darling son Jesus' name. Amen

Your Child & Servant,

Stephanie

CHAPTER ONE

FOR THIS *child* **I PRAYED** *and* **THE LORD HAS** *granted* **ME MY PETITION THAT I MADE TO** *Him*

1 Samuel 1:27 (ESV)

Desiring children for me was a long time dream. My husband and I wanted girl/boy twins, and we had already selected the name London as our daughter's name, and Joshua as our son's name. As a family, we already knew the adjustments that we would have to make to welcome children into our lives.

As my husband and I began preparing for my retirement from the United States Army, my husband was already retired from the United States Marine Corps and working as a government contractor. We figured that it would be the right time to start a family. At the time, I was an active duty Captain serving as a logistics officer for the 781st Military Intelligence Battalion at Fort Meade, Maryland. I had served my country sixteen years. Having a child earlier in my career although manageable was never an option for me because active duty military life can be difficult to navigate as a parent. Being a parent was so important to me that I did not want to miss birthdays, holidays, or significant events in my children's lives. I wanted to be able to be a full-time wife and mother. We tried naturally for six months to have a baby. Although that isn't considered a long time, my Obstetrician-Gynecologist (OBGYN) recommended because of our ages (I was 36 and my husband was 43) that we have testing done to see if anything was preventing us from conceiving naturally

Going to the reproductive specialist for the first time was very intense. We did our best to comfort each other, knowing that neither one of us wanted to be the reason we couldn't or wouldn't conceive a child. The reproductive specialist completed the Hysterosalpingogram (HSG)

Test for Blocked Fallopian Tubes and discovered that my tubes were blocked. The doctors reassured me that we still had options to become parents. The first option we were given was surgery, but the doctor advised against this option because of the scarring that could take place during the healing process. The scarring alone could possibly delay us from conceiving naturally for a year or more. The next option discussed was In Vitro Fertilization (IVF). IVF did not guarantee that we would be parents, but the reproductive specialist saw it as one of the more viable options at the time. Our initial IVF appointment was scheduled for the following week.

Our appointment was at Walter Reed National Military Medical Center in Bethesda, Maryland where they partnered with the A.R.T Institute of Washington to help military personnel hoping to conceive. The initial appointment involved a presentation in an auditorium with 70 other people. First, we were briefed on the timeline of IVF, the test that needed to happen before our cycle starting, and the cost associated with IVF. While sitting in the auditorium, I remember feeling a sense of peace and reassurance that we were not the only couple having difficulty conceiving. The second part of the appointment was a one-on-one meeting with the doctor to outline our individual test requirements, IVF cycle start date, and our initial payment. My husband and I were very fortunate because our primary care doctor had already ordered all of our tests, which made it possible to start taking birth control the following week, which meant we were officially on the IVF journey.

When I arrived home that night, the first thing I did

was pray. In prayer, I was vulnerable and transparent with God about the hurts of my past and my desire to be a mother. I desired to provide my children with all of the love, care, security, and compassion I lacked as a child. I remember praying for my twins London and Joshua that God would make them both healthy, wealthy, and wise. I prayed that He would allow them to arrive with ten fingers and ten toes, and hearts beating strong and, and I knew that God heard every prayer.

As you enter into this journey and you are praying for God to bless you with a child for you to love, nurture, provide and care for, Please know that God is listening to the prayers of your heart. He will give you peace and comfort as He strengthens your faith.

Let us pray

Heavenly Father,

Thank you for your grace and mercies that are new every morning. Lord, I come to you today asking you for the strength to endure whatever you have on the path before me. I know what it is that I desire for my life. Through prayer, I have made those requests known to you. I ask that you give me what I need to hold on to my faith until you bless me. Having faith when I experience heartbreak is not very easy, especially when it comes at a time when I want something so much that I can't think of anything else. During the times when my faith begins to waiver, and I feel weak, allow me to think of the other difficult times in my life when you showed up and worked the situation out just when I felt like all hope was lost.

Even though I do not fully understand why I had to experience infertility, I do know that you know and understand that this journey is a part of a plan that is bigger than me. I ask that you provide me with answers that give peace to my heart and mind. So many women are walking this same path from all over the world. I pray for each and every one of them. Heal them individually and collectively. Give them the desires of their hearts according to your will for their lives.

I Love You. I Adore you. I Trust You.

Yours Truly,
Stephanie

Today I am grateful for...

Personal Reflection from this prayer

Heavenly Father,

I come to you with my hands lifted up in praise thanking you for life, health, and strength. I am grateful that you watched over me during times of uncertainty. I have many things that are flooding my mind and my heart.

Help me to remember that you have given doctors knowledge and wisdom to help me conceive. You have blessed my body to be able to withstand the tests, medicines, and exams to endure this process. I am not forcing your hand Lord, IVF is one of your miracles. Only you can orchestrate something so amazing where I actually am able to see my babies before they are implanted in my body. I count it all joy that you have blessed me with a way to mother, a child.

I pray openly for the mental aspects of IVF. God, where there is confusion, give me clarity. Where there is hurt, provide me with understanding. Where there is heartache, give me Joy. Where there is weariness, give me strength. Where there is doubt, give me Hope. Lord, help me to see that you love me.

I place in your hands all that I am, and all that I desire to be.

I Love You. I Adore you. I Trust You.

Yours Truly,
Stephanie

Today I am grateful for...

Personal Reflection from this prayer

Heavenly Father,

I thank you for life, health, and strength. I know that you are a promise keeper. One of the promises that you made to me was that you would never leave nor forsake me. You have kept your promises. Lord, I need comfort, peace, love and joy that only you can give. As I prepare to go about my day, I ask that you accompany me during my appointments. Give me the right questions to ask that will ease my heart and mind. I need you to hear the cries of my heart and mend all of the places where discouragement has begun to set in.

I thank you in advance for my child, and I ask that during this time of waiting that you prepare me mentally, physically, emotionally and spiritually to be the parent that you have designed me to be.

I Love You. I Adore you. I Trust You.

Yours Truly,
Stephanie

Today I am grateful for...

Personal Reflection from this prayer

Heavenly Father,

    Thank you for the love I feel from you even when situations in my life are not what I hoped they would be. Today, I ask for peace of mind as my mind is raging like the wind back and forth. I need your restoration for the times that I feel as though I can not take another step. I need your joy in exchange for my pain. Provide me with renewed faith for areas that I am lacking faith. Allow my heart to draw so close to you that our hearts beat as one. You are my God, and I am your child, and today I place all I have and all I desire in your hands. Lord, no matter where I am on this IVF journey allow me to feel your presence like never before. Reassure me that I am walking the path that you would have me to walk.

I Love You. I Adore you. I Trust You.

Yours Truly,
Stephanie

Today I am grateful for...

Personal Reflection from this prayer

Heavenly Father,

    I come into your presence this day with love in my heart for you that is difficult to explain and comprehend. Today, I give you the very best that I have to give in prayer not because I want anything from you but because of everything you have done in my life up to this point. I am grateful for life, health, and strength. I am grateful for your unconditional love that comforts me when all hell is breaking loose in my mind. I am grateful for your light that shines in the darkest places in my life. I am grateful for friends who are closer than family, assisting me through this journey. I am grateful for your provisions during this infertility process. Although doors have closed in my face at times, you have opened new doors and windows of opportunity, and for that, I am genuinely grateful. Lord today, I ask for nothing but pause to thank you for EVERYTHING humbly.

I Love You. I Adore you. I Trust You.

Yours Truly,
Stephanie

Today I am grateful for...

Personal Reflection from this prayer

CHAPTER TWO

BEFORE I FORMED *you* IN THE WOMB I KNEW YOU *before* *you were* BORN I *set* YOU APART I APPOINTED YOU AS A PROPHET TO THE NATIONS

Jeremiah 1: 5 (NIV)

Honestly, before I started my IVF journey, I had never paid particular attention to Jeremiah 1:5 that states, "Before I formed you in the womb I knew you." It helped me to comprehend that in the same way God knew me before I was formed in the womb, He knows the twins that I long to conceive.

Starting IVF delivered mixed emotions. Taking birth control pills to start my menstrual cycle was a simple process. The injectable medication to stimulate the ovaries to produce eggs was more of a challenge. Having to give myself four shots a day at scheduled times in different parts of my stomach was very uncomfortable and painful. Desiring a child made the injection worth it, but my hormones were all over the place. During this process, which lasts 10-12 days, I had to report to Walter Reed every other day to see how many follicles could be seen during the vaginal ultrasound.

The follicle count helps the doctors to decide if I should increase or decrease the dosage of my medication. By my third appointment, I felt discouraged because my follicle count was not growing. Honestly, I was tired of giving myself injections and my faith was beginning to weaken.

The emotional roller coaster during this time made me pray even more. During these mornings I thought my infertility was unfair because there were many women getting pregnant by accident. why me? What had I done wrong? And why would He make it so difficult to have a child? I had personally witnessed quite a few women have children that were unable to properly care for them. My husband and I are more than capable of providing for a child. It was then that God's word helped me to see that IVF was destined to be a part of my story before, even before I was born.

As I prayed and trusted God, my follicles began to increase in number and size. By the last day, I was ready for my trigger shot and egg retrieval. I'm unsure where you are in your IVF journey, what I know God knew you before you were formed in your mother's womb, and He knows you now

Let's go to God in Prayer.

Heavenly Father,

In your presence, I say thank you for all you are doing and all you are going to do. For allowing me to see another day in spite of how yesterday went, I am Grateful. Lord, I am standing before you with everything that I have to give, asking you to bless me with the desires of my heart. I have no one else to turn to accept you. I know that you are a God that changes the impossible into possible at a moments notice. I pray for myself and anyone I may have hurt in any way during this process. Infertility is a hard pill to swallow, it's even harder when I feel as though I am alone. Lord, allow me to remain encouraged even if I do not get the results I want. Help me to make wise decisions moving forward, be it deciding to do another IVF cycle or walk away. Sorting through my emotions is difficult. I give you the concerns of my heart.

In your word, John 14:1 says, "Let not your heart be troubled: ye believe in God, believe also in me." Today that is what I am doing, believing in you. At this moment I pray for any issues that occupy a spot in my heart and mind. God, give me closure where there is none. Quiet my mind when it's raging. My heart is in your hands for you to do your will. I ask that you keep me in perfect peace as I focus on all the things that I have to be grateful for at this moment.

I Love You. I Adore you. I Trust You.

Yours Truly,
Stephanie

Today I am grateful for...

Personal Reflection from this prayer

Heavenly and Gracious Father,

I kneel before you giving you everything I have to offer. My heart and my mind is consumed with having a family: my shots, my follicles, my trigger, transfer date, my beta numbers, and my ultrasound that I often forget to pause and enjoy life. God, come in and give me peace that only you can provide. Show me you are in control and that all things are working out for my good. God, remind me that you love me, and that you have plans for my life in spite of how the situation is at this moment. Cover all women experiencing this journey, and provide them with your peace.

I Love You. I Adore you. I Trust You.

Yours Truly,
Stephanie

Today I am grateful for...

Personal Reflection from this prayer

Heavenly Father,

    Thank you for life, health, and strength. Lord, in spite of how things look on the outside, you know the plans that you have for me. I have to admit that I do not understand all your plans or some of my pain, but my past has taught me to trust you, and that is what I am going to do. I surrender my heart, soul, mind, and my spirit so that you can have your way in my life. Allow me to find the silver linings in the darkest clouds so my faith will be renewed and restored continually. I pray for my family this morning that we build a bond that can't be broken, and we demonstrate unconditional love for one another that builds bridges. I am so in love with you Lord, and I thank you for loving me back.

I Love You. I Adore you. I Trust You.

Yours Truly,
Stephanie

Today I am grateful for...

Personal Reflection from this prayer

Heavenly Father,

Thank you for giving me life, health, and strength. Today, I have an appointment for my vaginal ultrasounds. I am nervous because I genuinely have no idea what to expect. God, cover my heart and mind during these appointments because these appointments could give me hope or break my heart. As I trust the hands and wisdom of the doctors, give me the questions to ask, the knowledge to understand what is being said, and the courage to speak up or seek a second opinion if something does not appear to be right.

If today is rough for me, teach me to be thankful for another day. Strengthen and clothe me in your love and power. Help me to pray for, uplift, and support others and myself.

I Love You. I Adore you. I Trust You.

Yours Truly,
Stephanie

Today I am grateful for...

Personal Reflection from this prayer

Heavenly Father,

As I rise this morning to start my day, I commit my day into your hands. Have your way in my life. You are an all-knowing God that knows my heart's desire even when I can not find the words, and for that I am grateful. Today I ask you for nothing, I realize that I have so much in life that I have to be grateful for.

I am grateful for life and the activity of my limbs. I am thankful for my family and friends. I am grateful that you allowed me to wake up, and pray from my heart. I am grateful for the people around me that give me hope, renew my faith, pray for me, help me to not feel lonely, answer questions, and give me support that I never thought possible. I am grateful that even though infertility is part of my life journey, there are some options available to have a family. I am grateful that this journey has opened my heart and mind to understand that it's nothing I did to cause my infertility. I am grateful that I AM HERE.

As I close this prayer, I leave all that I am and desire to be in your hands. I humbly surrender to you in exchange for your peace as you work out the details of my life.

I Love You. I Adore you. I Trust You.

Yours Truly,
Stephanie

Today I am grateful for...

Personal Reflection from this prayer

CHAPTER THREE

For nothing is impossible with God

Luke 1:37 (NLT)

The next phase of IVF for me was beautiful and confirmed to me that God can do the impossible. I was finally ready for my trigger shot. The trigger shot happens thirty-six before egg retrieval and informs the body to release the eggs for the embryologist. On my way to the hospital I thanked God for allowing me to make it this far, and reminded myself that the number of eggs retrieved doesn't matter, it only takes one fertilized implanted egg to have a baby.

When we arrived at Walter Reed hospital the retrieval team, doctors, and the anesthesiologist came into my room to brief my husband and I about what would occur. They went into detail about how they would retrieve the eggs while my husband was in another location providing a sperm sample. I remember joking with my husband about not coming out of the room too fast with the sperm sample. The next thing I remember is waking up with the number eight on the back of my hand. The number eight was the number of eggs they retrieved. After I was awake and alert, the doctors informed me that the next step was combining the sperm and the egg for the fertilization to occur. How many eggs that are fertilized during this process is indeed up to God. I prayed and told God that I trust Him and I am grateful to make it to this day.

On day four the doctors called my husband and I to inform us that we had one egg that survived and that we need to report the next morning for our embryo transfer. Arriving at my transfer appointment was exciting. As we entered our, embryologist gave us a picture of our embryo that was being transferred. This was the first time in my life that I experienced love at first sight. Watching the monitor while our embryo was being transferred was magical. I thank God because I realized at that moment that with God, all things are possible. After the transfer was complete, the embryologist briefed my husband and I to take it easy for the next two weeks. Now the two-week wait began.

Remembering that nothing is impossible with God helped me to have hope and faith in times of doubt. May you not forget that even though it may appear impossible, it is not impossible if you trust God.

Let's approach the Throne of Grace.

Heavenly Father,

I come to you with love and adoration. I thank you for covering me with your love, grace, and mercy. Today, I lay my heart at your feet for you to have your way. There are so many things that race through my mind daily. I need you to still my mind so that I can pray to you, turn over all of my concerns to you, and patiently wait for you to answer.

I pray for those families that are on the brink of falling apart because this journey to parenthood is taking a toll. Lord wrap them in your arms and give them the words that express the love they feel for one another, build bonds, restore joy, and bless them according to your will for their lives.

I am also asking for prayer for the women in IVF, whose donor eggs, surrogacy, or adoption have ended negatively. As they begin to mend their lives back together give them direction, peace, and strength to make significant decisions for their lives. In Luke 1:37 the bible says …'For with God nothing shall be impossible'. Today, I have the Faith to know that in spite of how it looks you will do the impossible in my life.

I Love You. I Adore you. I Trust You.

Yours Truly,
Stephanie

Today I am grateful for...

Personal Reflection from this prayer

Heavenly Father,

I come to you saying thank you for rising with all power in your hands. I thank you for loving me the way that you do. I thank you for the price that you paid on Calvary for me. I thank you for giving me life, health, and strength. I cry out to you Lord asking when is it going to be my turn to be a mother. When are you going to fulfill your promise to me? When will I see the results of my heartfelt prayers? Lord, as I cry out to you show me your Glory, and begin to shift things into place for my good. I thank you for the understanding that in spite of how it may look that you are still a prayer answering God. Allow me to enjoy my family today while I remember that you are behind the scenes working everything out on my behalf. There are times when I am struggling emotionally, and today I ask that you give me peace that surpasses all understanding.

As I close in prayer, I need you to know Lord, that even in my darkest of days you are my hope and I do not take your love and your miracles for granted.

I Love You. I Adore you. I Trust You.

Yours Truly,
Stephanie

Today I am grateful for...

Personal Reflection from this prayer

Heavenly Father,

I love you more than anything. Thank you for allowing me to see another day filled with so many possibilities. Today, I commit all my hurt, doubt, joy, pain, my lack of understanding, my desire to be a mom, my marriage, everything involving me into your hand for you to do you will. Lord in spite of how I feel I choose to fill my heart with Joy.

I choose to allow the love that you have for me to cover my heart and my mind. I choose to love myself, flaws and all. I choose to pray about my infertility instead of worrying every time my spirit becomes cloudy with what-ifs. I choose today as an emotional day off from IVF so that I can clearly see all of the other things in my life that I have to be grateful for. I choose to make time to thank you for the little things that I have overlooked lately on this journey. I choose to trust you with all matters concerning me.

I pray for the women this morning that are experiencing any type of pain, be it physical, spiritual, mental, or emotional because they need you. Their hearts are crying out to you, even though they may not have the words. Lord, examine their hearts to give them that peace and comfort that only you can provide.

I Love You. I Adore you. I Trust You.

Yours Truly,
Stephanie

Today I am grateful for...

Personal Reflection from this prayer

Heavenly and Gracious Father,

I come into your presence today merely to thank you. With so much chaos in the world, I am grateful that I still have my health, life, and strength. Today reminded me that even though things may not be the way that I have anticipated I am still here, and for that I thank you.

Remind me today of your unfailing love for me. Remind me today that you are God and that you have everything in control. Remind me today that you are always present with me even at my lowest times. Remind me that you are a God who fulfills his promise time and time again. Remind me that in you I can find peace when the storms of life are raging. I thank you in advance for all that you have done and will continue to do.

I Love You. I Adore you. I Trust You.

Yours Truly,
Stephanie

Today I am grateful for...

Personal Reflection from this prayer

Heavenly Father,

I thank you for life and the ability to come to you in prayer. Lord, cover me as I wait on different test results. Waiting on eggs counts, the number of eggs retrieved, the number of eggs that survived for fertilization is so nerve-wracking for me because I can not control the outcome.

You are God, and I know that you love and care for me, and you have a plan for my life. When your plan doesn't line up with the plan I have in my mind and heart, please allow me to not lose faith, but hold on to the fact that you are God. I know that you love me more than anything in this world.

I Love You. I Adore you. I Trust You.

Yours Truly,
Stephanie

Today I am grateful for...

Personal Reflection from this prayer

CHAPTER FOUR

Trust in the LORD with all your heart, and do not lean on your own understanding.

Proverbs 3:5 (ESV)

The process of IVF is tough for me to explain to anyone. IVF is one of those things that you have to experience to fully understand. Even then, your experience will vary from others who are still in the process.

The two-week wait after our embryo transfer felt like forever. Throughout the two weeks, I took it easy and prayed that God would do His will. I prayed for my twins to implant and begin to grow. My friend, Jennifer, flew in from California to hold my hand and assure that I rested. She waited on me hand and foot. Around day- eight post embryo transfer, I was tempted to take a pregnancy test, but I resisted the urge I did not want to be stressed wondering if I tested too early; therefore I decided to wait until we had our HCG test, also known as the beta test.

The morning of our test, my husband and I were both very nervous because this is our moment of truth. Before we got in the car, we prayed together, and I felt a sense of peace that was hard to understand and explain. When we arrived at the lab, we drew a number and waited to be escorted back. The nurse that did the labs informed us that within the next four-hours a nurse from the fertility team would call us with our results.

When I got the call that my beta test results were negative and I was not pregnant I was numb. In my mind, I went over every day of my two-week wait to think if there was something that I could have or should have done differently. I had done everything that I possibly could. My thoughts then shifted to my prayers.

Initially, I had a hard time comprehending why God did not answer my prayers. I knew so many couples and single women who did not want children that were pregnant and had no difficulty or complications conceiving. I remember going into my bedroom and realizing that although I wanted to scream at the top of my lungs, I couldn't. Instead, I sat on the floor and wept. I wept for my unborn children, my husband, and then myself. I felt as though all my prayers had gone unheard. My mind was going a mile a minute with questions like, what is the next step? How long do I have to wait to start another IVF cycle? Am I going to do another IVF cycle? I was a ball of emotions and uncertainty for the next few days.

By the time our follow-up appointment took place, my husband and I decided we were not going to do another IVF cycle immediately to give my body a break. Emotionally we were drained, but our faith was strong. It was time to rest and regroup.

This portion of the book is indeed the hardest for me to write because I do not want you to get discouraged or feel as though God is not listening to you because He is. The peace and comfort I felt during this time is evidence of how God heard my prayers. Am I disappointed? Absolutely. Am I hurt and emotional? Yes! But even more than that, I am just curious about where God will take me in the next chapter of my life. You will overcome negative results in due time. What is important is that you are honest about how you feel, and your thoughts. When your heart and mind are in the right place, then proceed to the next step.

Let's make our petitions known to God.

Heavenly Father,

I come before you saying thank you for the love that you have shown to me, not only for right now but in the past as well. I am in a place where I need you more than ever. Infertility is a different experience for everyone. Allow me to be able to communicate with compassion and understanding. Teach me the words to say that heal and restore hope.

Lord, I am suffering from depression in a significant way because I feel like a failure. This process has ripped me to my core. Lord, hear the cry of my heart this morning as I ask you to comfort me right now, wrap your love around me, help me not to feel alone. Remind me of times in my past where things started out rough, and you worked everything out for me. Remind me at this moment that you have never left me nor forsaken me. Reveal to me that you do have a plan for my life, although it's not happening the way that I want it to, you are working behind the scenes.

Strengthen me so that I can begin to have hope again. Surround me with people who can speak life into me. Thank you in advance for not only hearing my prayer but for answering. Heal my heavy heart. Provide peace and comfort. Allow your love to be shared today even if it's in a small way.

I Love You. I Adore you. I Trust You.

Yours Truly,
Stephanie

Today I am grateful for...

Personal Reflection from this prayer

Heavenly Father,

Thank you for your faithfulness, grace, and mercy towards me. Lord, I ask that if the doctors give me news that may break my heart, that you will give me Godly wisdom to seek a second opinion before I throw in the towel. I know that even though you have given doctors' wisdom, they are human. Ultimately you have the last say for what transpires in my life. At this moment I am hanging on by a string to my last ounce of faith. I need you to intervene right now. As I continue into this day, I ask that you give me peace in my heart and mind.

Lord, I give you the hurting me, the broken me, the strong me, the confused me, the crying me, the depressed me so that you can put me back together the way that you see fit so I can continue on the path that you have set before me.

I Love You. I Adore you. I Trust You.

Yours Truly,
Stephanie

Today I am grateful for...

Personal Reflection from this prayer

Heavenly Father,

Thank you for your love, your grace, and your mercy. As I start this day, I commit it to your hands for you to do your will. Lord, I am asking for joy down in my soul that can only be given by you. I have been so busy with everything IVF, and although that isn't a bad thing, I am asking you today to show me how to take an emotional day off. A day where I just think of all the other things in my life that I have to be grateful for, and all of the blessings that are indeed headed my way.

Help me today to be grateful for all the miracles that you have performed in my life up to this point. Help me to be grateful for the little things that make a huge difference in the lives of others. Help me to be grateful for the love that I feel from those around me. Help me to be grateful for the gift of life, that many take for granted. Help me to be grateful for the ability to pray, and the faith to know that you are a prayer-answering God. Allow me to sit back and take it all in because you are God, and you love me more than I can comprehend.

I Love You. I Adore you. I Trust You.

Yours Truly,
Stephanie

Today I am grateful for...

Personal Reflection from this prayer

Heavenly Father,

Thank you for the opportunity to come into your presence knowing that you hear the cry of my heart. I have so much going on, not only in my life but in my heart and my mind. I need you to help me balance all of the things going on in my life so that I do not miss the essential little things in my search for something big.

Show me what to do while I am waiting for you to answer my prayers to give me the children I desire. I do not want to take anything that you give me for granted so allow me to find things to be grateful for every day and humble me and remind me that you promised never to leave nor forsake me. I am in your hands, and I know you have everything I need.

I Love You. I Adore you. I Trust You.

Yours Truly,
Stephanie

Today I am grateful for...

Personal Reflection from this prayer

Heavenly Father,

I am thankful to you for freedom in every area of my life. I place my desire to start a family at your feet. I am grateful for the peace in my heart knowing you love and care for me. There are many situations and different scenarios in the IVF process that need your attention. I ask that you address all of those situations in a way that only you can.

I thank you for your presence in my life. I can not always feel you, but I do know you are with me through the best and worst of times. Before you give me the child I desire, I pray for them now that they are healthy, wealthy, and wise. Allow their heartbeat to be strong, their bones to be healthy. Allow their internal organs to function as they should. Allow them to make it from retrieval to birth.

I Love You. I Adore you. I Trust You.

Yours Truly,
Stephanie

Today I am grateful for...

Personal Reflection from this prayer

CHAPTER FIVE

For I know the plans I have for you, declares the Lord, plans to prosper and not to harm you, plans to give you hope and a future.

Jeremiah 29:11 (NIV)

"For I know the plans I have for you, declares the Lord, plans to prosper you and not harm you, plans to give you hope and a future" Jeremiah 29:11. This is the scripture that has always governed my life. Knowing and understanding that God knows the plans He has for me strengthens me and renews my faith. Moving beyond my negative beta results was a difficult road to navigate, but it was the only option I had.

Every morning I would ask myself different questions about my IVF process. I decided to compile a list of questions for the doctor so my husband and I could make sound decisions about our next step from an informed place instead of an emotional one. During our appointment, our doctor sincerely apologized for our loss. With patience and compassion, he answered all of our questions reassuring us that there was nothing that could have been done differently.

Our decision as a couple not to go immediately into another IVF cycle was understood by our doctor because he was keenly aware of the mental, physical, emotional, and financial impacts of IVF. After we completed our appointment, my husband and I decided to give ourselves six-months of recovery before making any decisions about our next course of action. Essentially, we had three options to consider: (1) do another IVF cycle, (2) adopt, or (3) console ourselves with the fact that we would not be parents.

Over the next few months, we dealt with some emotionally rough times. Two weeks after our failed IVF cycle, I began experiencing intense neck and shoulder pain. I assumed I was just internalizing everything that had happened and the stress was just overwhelming me. That indeed was not the case. I went to the emergency room for testing. I was diagnosed with three herniated discs in my neck that were pressing down on a nerve. The doctor prescribed narcotics and steroids that I had to take for one month, and then we would access if surgery was needed.

Two months after my IVF, my husband and I relocated to Atlanta, Georgia. On my journey of forgiving God for my experiences, I had started to rebuild my relationship with my mother. I sent for my mother to come and help us unpack the boxes and organize our new house. Thinking back, I realized how much God loves me because my mother and I had the opportunity to have long and engaging conversations the day she arrived. We had a chance to express our love for each other, and I expressed my forgiveness and unconditional love for her. That night my mother went upstairs and never came down because she unbelievably passed away in her sleep. I felt as though my heart had been ripped from my body.

A couple of months after my mother's funeral, I decided to go into therapy to help me deal with my uncontrollable floods of emotions. One day after a therapy appointment, I was on the couch and the scripture Jeremiah 29:11 crossed my mind. I tried to dismiss the thought of the scripture because I was not on speaking terms with God. For the next two weeks every thought I had focused on Jeremiah 29:11, so much so that I found it hard to sleep. I remember thinking Lord, what is your plan? Please show me because all I have felt is the pain. That night I took my phone and read every version of the scripture that I could find.

As the nights turned into days, I distinctly remember feeling less depressed and less emotional. The pain finally lifted. As I talked to God, I realized that had I been pregnant, I would not have been able to take the medication that helped me to get well. At that moment I also realized had I miscarried after my mother's death, I would have blamed myself, and God would not have wanted me to accept blame for something beyond my control.

The beautiful thing about this scripture is that it does not promise me that I am not going to have hard times in life. Nor does it guarantee that everything is going to go my way, however, it does reassure me that God has a plan for my life and that plan will give me hope and a future.

IVF is challenging in more ways than one. The unique thing about IVF is that it may not challenge you in the manner that it challenged me. Nonetheless, you will be challenged. During the time that you are tested I want you to remember that God knows the plans He has for you, and those plans are to prosper you and not harm you. Those plans are there to give you hope and a future. Please remember if there is hope in the future, there is power in the present.

Let's go to God about His plans for our life.

Heavenly Father,

I come before you to thank you for your loving-kindness toward me not just today but always. As I prepare for another day God, I ask that you prepare my heart, mind, body, and spirit for the things that come my way. Allow me to handle different situations with grace and integrity. While trying to have a baby, I have become so consumed. Today I ask that you show me all areas in my life where I need to create balance or focus. While on this journey, infertility seems to be the topic of almost every conversation that I have or the thing that my mind continues to focus on. Surround me with people who understand this IVF phase of my life and are willing to listen.

Father God, I ask that you comfort the hearts of the women around me who are seeking answers about their lives and the direction they need to go in. Suffering any kind of loss or disappointment is hard and it knocks us off balance. I am asking you God to ground their feet, dry their tears, and provide them with peace and direction. As your direction for them becomes clear Lord, I ask that you continue to meet all their needs. You are worthy of the Glory and the Honor. God, there is someone whose faith is wavering because of all the rough things she has been through in life, and now on top everything, she is having infertility issues. Lord, she and other women, are questioning your presence in their lives, I am asking that you begin rebuilding their faith today. Show them, that even though it has been rough, you have never left their side. Also when they lacked, you still provided for their basic needs. Lord, I thank you for my life and the angels that protect me.

I Love You. I Adore you. I Trust You.

Yours Truly,
Stephanie

Today I am grateful for...

Personal Reflection from this prayer

Heavenly Father,

I stand in awe of you today for all the grace and mercy you have always shown me. Lord, I give you my heart, my mind, my soul, and my desires because you and you alone know the plans you have for me and my significant other, both individually and collectively. I pray today for my significant other that I do not lose sight of their love and support for me while working toward my heart's desire to have a baby. As I go through this day, I ask you to give me peace that only you can.

There are many women on this journey with me, so I stop and pray for them. For those who have suffered loss and don't know which way to turn, I ask that you help them find the direction and guidance for moving forward. For the women who have become pregnant, allow them to enjoy their pregnancies without the overwhelming concern of miscarriage. Provide peace to all of us, that only you can give.

I Love You. I Adore you. I Trust You.

Yours Truly,
Stephanie

Today I am grateful for...

Personal Reflection from this prayer

Heavenly Father,

    Thank you for all the fantastic things you have done in my life. For the times you have protected me with your loving-kindness and tender mercies. I understand that you have given doctors the wisdom and the knowledge to bless me with the family I have always wanted, so help me to remain focused.

    Lord, you do everything in your perfect timing. I need to know that I am not taking my body, heart, and mind through this if your intent was for me not to have a child or children. Even though that answer would hurt me to my core, it's better than the continuous heartbreak from negative results. Lord, I ask you to cover the women on this journey with me. Many of them have heavy hearts for various reasons. I pray you carry all of our burdens, heartache, body pain, mental anguish, and lack of faith and turn it into strength, love, joy, hope, and peace. Allow celebrations of life to take place for the women who have received great news. Allow them not to operate in fear but enjoy their blessings one heartbeat at a time.

    You are such an amazing God, who does fantastic things.

I Love You. I Adore you. I Trust You.

Yours Truly,
Stephanie

Today I am grateful for...

Personal Reflection from this prayer

Heavenly Father,

I come into your presence thanking and praising you with the desires of my heart and soul knowing that you care enough for me to listen to my prayers. At this moment I need you to place your angels around me keeping me safe from all hurt, harm, and danger. I am depending on you to protect me. Yesterday, I received news that I have multiple fibroids. This is devastating because of the pain that I feel in my heart. Allow me to see that I am human and that the emotions I am feeling are real, that I am allowed to feel this way. During this time I ask that you strengthen me and let me be still while you give me guidance on what I am to do next. I know that you do not desire this process of bearing a child to break me mentally, emotionally, spiritually, or financially. I am trusting that you can and will perform a miracle.

My heart is aching with pain, that I never knew I could feel. Heal me, Lord, as only you can. The life you have called me to live has so many ups and downs, twist and turns but you have kept me through more than this. I know you have not left me to walk this road alone. I just need to be transparent so my heart does not become hardened. Even as I cry out to you from the pits of my heart, I know that you have all power in your hands and I need to see your power manifest in this situation.

I Love You. I Adore you. I Trust You.

Yours Truly,
Stephanie

Today I am grateful for...

Personal Reflection from this prayer

Heavenly Father,

Thank you for all you have done and all you are going to do. Today I ask you, God, to cover me from the crown of my head to the sole of my feet. This journey has tested my faith to the ultimate limit. I ask that you build my faith in ways I never imagined. Provide me with peace that surpasses my own understanding.

At this moment I pause to pray for other women on the IVF journey. I pray for the woman that feels as though she has given all that she is able. Give her hope to keep moving forward. Allow her to see that your plan and your timing are perfect. For the woman who has been told that donor eggs are her only option. I ask you to help her see that the baby will be hers and she will love her baby above what she thought possible. For the woman who has received gut-wrenching news, I ask that she understand a delay is not denial.

Jeremiah 29:11 is your promise to us, and it states: "For I know the plans I have for you, declares the Lord, plans for good and not for evil, to give you a future and a hope." With you guiding the path of our future, I have hope I never thought possible.

I Love You, I Adore you, and I Trust You.

Yours Truly,
Stephanie

Today I am grateful for...

Personal Reflection from this prayer

CHAPTER SIX

He heals the brokenhearted and binds up their wounds

Psalms 147:3 (NIV)

Deciding what decision to make following our failed IVF cycle was not easy. Starting another cycle with no guarantee was hard to fathom. Adoption, although a beautiful option for us and a deserving child, produced fear in my husband and I. Our minds filled with questions about the child possibly wanting to know his or her biological parents. For us, that was a lot to deal with emotionally. Accepting the fact that we would not be parents was not an option either. The one thing my husband and I did know was that we were not in a hurry to make a decision.

In my life, I have experienced situations that have made me stronger, and wiser. IVF was essentially no different. My failed cycle helped me to find the courage to start the healing process that would forever change my life. I decided to seek therapy to manage my hurt. Therapy created a turning point in my life. My newfound courage allowed me to come face to face with all of the hidden pain of molestation, abandonment, abuse, and the feelings of inadequacy that I intentionally avoided or repressed. As I went through my therapy sessions, I no longer thought of having a child as a way to rectify all of the hurt I experienced in my childhood. Through mindfulness practices, meditation and prayer, I was able to embrace the fact that God was healing my broken heart and binding up my wounds.

At this moment in my life, IVF is no longer an option for me. My Fibroid pain became so severe my husband and I decided I should have a hysterectomy. Before having my hysterectomy, the doctor informed me that my ovaries would remain in case my husband and I wanted to have a baby via a surrogate. After all I have endured during this journey being a mother is still an option. God changed what my plan looked like, but the doors have not completely closed on motherhood. Many people would assume that my Faith would weaken, but in fact my faith is stronger than it has ever been.

The ability to heal and live from a place of peace is why you are holding this book in your hands. I had to experience IVF personally to understand the process. The peace, understanding, hope, and faith prayer provides has given me a profound desire to pray for women on this infertility journey. I want other women to not lose hope or faith in an amazing God that can do the impossible.

Regardless of where you are mentally and emotionally at this moment, there is healing for any area of your life. God can and will use your challenges and disappointments to help you and others to heal in a way that you never imagined. I simply ask you to trust him.

Let's go to God in prayer.

Heavenly Father,

Thank you for your presence that surrounds me with peace I can not comprehend. Lord, I struggle a every time I hear a woman share that she got pregnant without trying. I am happy for her, but I can't help but wonder when it's going to be my turn. Lord, give me direction for moving forward. As I navigate through my options through this infertility journey, go before me and open doors to prevent me from throwing in the towel and becoming weary.

I openly admit Lord, that I get worn out in so many ways that I am barely holding on. The dream of embracing my child in my arms is too strong for me to let go. I pray for other women at this moment. Go into the hearts of the women who are suffering in silence. The women who have no one they can talk to or depend on. God, please send them comfort and allow them to see that they are not alone. Send them precisely what they need. For those who have marriages or relationships that are on the verge of falling apart, I ask that you begin the restoration process that will make their marriages and relationships stronger than ever.

Lord, everything I am and all I desire to be, I give to you for you to do your will.

I Love You. I Adore you. I Trust You.

Yours Truly,
Stephanie

Today I am grateful for...

Personal Reflection from this prayer

Heavenly Father,

I want to thank you for all the love I feel from you even when situations in my life are not what I hoped they would be. Today I ask for your peace as my mind rages back and forth. I pray for your comfort for the days that my heart is broken. I need restoration for the times I feel as though I can not take another step. I need your joy in exchange for my pain. Please provide me with renewed faith for areas where I am lacking.

Allow my heart to draw so close to you that our hearts beat as one. You are my God, and I am your child. Today I place all I have and all I desire in your hands. Lord, no matter where I am on this IVF journey allow me to feel your presence like never before. Reassure me that I am walking the path that you would have me to walk.

I Love You. I Adore you. I Trust You.

Yours Truly,
Stephanie

Today I am grateful for...

Personal Reflection from this prayer

Heavenly Father,

Today I am simply grateful. I am grateful that throughout the day you keep a hedge of protection around me. I am grateful you love me with a love that is often hard to comprehend, but know it exists. I am grateful for my faith that seems to get renewed right in the nick of time. I am grateful for the strength I find right when I am on the verge of giving up.

Lord, continue to cover me as I deal with infertility physically, spiritually, financially, mentally and emotionally. I know that you are going to answer my prayers in your way and in your time. I am grateful that I can cast my cares upon you because you care for me.

I Love You. I Adore you. I Trust You.

Yours Truly,
Stephanie

Today I am grateful for...

Personal Reflection from this prayer

Heavenly and Gracious Father,

    I come to you gladly giving you the desires of my heart for you to do your will. God strengthen me for the road ahead. I am at a standstill because I am trying to figure out which direction to go in next. My heart is divided because even though I desire a child in the worst way, I am hurting because of the loss that I have endured during this IVF journey. Lord, I know that you have perfect timing and a plan. I ask that you continue to show up in my life in small ways. Show me your will for my life as it pertains to infertility.

I Love You. I Adore you. I Trust You.

Yours Truly,
Stephanie

Today I am grateful for...

Personal Reflection from this prayer

Heavenly and Gracious Father,

Thank you for all the blessings you have given me. I am thankful that you love me the way that you do. The love that you have given me I do not comprehend, but I can feel it. I ask that you mend my heart in areas that I cannot see. My heart has been broken many times on this journey. God, although I know you are in complete control, there are times when I have doubted or just didn't understand the plan for my life.

I acknowledge that you love me. However, I do not always feel your presence when the answers are not what I desired. Lord, you are faithful, and I need you to keep me faithful no matter how infertility challenges me. I will wait for you.

I Love You. I Adore you. I Trust You.

Yours Truly,
Stephanie

Today I am grateful for...

Personal Reflection from this prayer

CHAPTER SEVEN

pray without ceasing

1 Thessalonians 5:17 (KJV)

Learning to pray without ceasing reminds me of my great grandmother Beulah Holt. I remember her telling me that interceding for others is the most powerful form of prayer. Honestly, I am not sure how it transpired, but praying for others while I need prayer myself has become very natural to me and it is a significant part of who I am. When I first entered the IVF journey the prayers that God placed on my heart surprised me. The peace and comfort God provided through prayers I shared with other women was mind-blowing. Helping other women find hope on days when they felt all hope was lost is a beautiful feeling that I will never be able to describe adequately.

The following prayers are here for you to pray for other women who are on the IVF journey with you. IVF connects us with other women in a way you wouldn't ever imagine. All of us share the desire of starting a family or making our families bigger. No one understands this process unless you experience it up close and personal as we have. As we go to God for our sisters and the desires of their hearts, it is my prayer that you are blessed beyond what you can comprehend.

May you be divinely connected to the women that come to mind as you pray. I pray that these prayers allow you to find common ground by which you can support others when they need it the most.

Let's approach the throne of Grace.

Today I am grateful for...

Personal Reflection from this prayer

Heavenly Father,

We thank you for your loving-kindness and tender mercies toward us. We acknowledge that we need you and that we are nothing without you. We ask you to prepare us for the children that we are praying for.

Your promises are real in our lives, and we know that you can and will do anything but fail. For those of us who are struggling mentally with infertility, we ask that you show us the way ahead so that we are able to hold on with everything that we have. We desire the sound of little feet running through our homes, and the day when our child will call us mommy. Hear the cries of our hearts and souls and send your angels to guide us on this journey.

We Love You. We Adore you. We Trust You.

Yours Truly,
Stephanie

Today I am grateful for...

Personal Reflection from this prayer

Heavenly and Gracious Father,

We come saying thank you. Thank you for the love that you have shown us. We had been told we are unable to conceive on our own. Lord, we ask you for the strength to continue regardless of the obstacles that we will come in contact with.

We are asking you for your loving-kindness to enter our hearts while we are on this journey. Today, we ask that you give someone the financial breakthrough that they need to continue on this journey, that they believe the promises that you made to them. I am also asking for true miracles. I am praying that you allow women to conceive naturally even though it would be impossible medically. And I pray that you are glorified as it is only you who could perform such an amazing miracle in their lives.

Lord, as we go through this day, we just want you to know that we are yours. We are thankful that you promised to hide us in the safety of your arms at all times.

We Love You. We Adore You. We Trust You.

Yours Truly,
Stephanie

Today I am grateful for...

Personal Reflection from this prayer

Heavenly Father,

Come into our hearts and give us your love, peace of mind, faith, wisdom and hope. Emotions on this journey are often high, and it is in those times that we realize how much we really want to be mothers. We are asking that in these times you draw us closer to you so we don't forget that you have a plan for our lives. You are working things out in our lives in your perfect timing.

Today we place our infertility in your hands for you to do your will. This act is a testament to our faith because we are accustomed to being in control of our lives. We are trusting and leaning on you for the path ahead. Continue to strengthen our relationships with our significant others and our families because we believe that a family that prays together stays together. Lord, have your way in our lives.

We Love You. We Adore you. We Trust You.

Yours Truly,
Stephanie

Today I am grateful for...

Personal Reflection from this prayer

Heavenly Father,

We come to you with everything that we have in us, asking you to do your will in our lives. Lord, there are a lot of women who are taking their beta pregnancy test to find out if their dreams are about to become a reality. As we know, some are going to get great news, and others are going to have broken hearts.

For the women who are told that they are not pregnant, I ask that you cover them and begin to heal their broken hearts immediately. Some of them are going to feel betrayed by you and angry because they feel they've done all that they could and nothing went a they had planned. Please Lord, comfort them and show them that you haven't forgotten them and that you are going to give them what you promised in due time.

For the women who find out that they are pregnant, cover them as well because they have entered a new stage of worry that won't end until the baby is safely embraced in their arms. Lord, we all ask that you protect our hearts from fear and worry because you will provide everything like you have done so many times before.

We Love You. We Adore you. We Trust You.

Yours Truly,
Stephanie

Today I am grateful for...

Personal Reflection from this prayer

Heavenly Father,

We thank you for the peace that only you can give to us. With everything we experienced in trying to conceive a child, this journey has dominated our lives. If it's not appointments, it's shots, if it's not shots, it's our follicle number and size. The concern then shifts to how many eggs will be retrieved, then the egg quality. Next, we worry about the transfer, and the nerve-wracking two weeks' wait. Even though it should stop there, it becomes the ultrasounds ,not just one, but every one because we are consumed with our babies arriving safely. If we find out it didn't work, we question ourselves and You because we just don't understand.

Today we ask that you reveal to us all of the other amazing things that you have placed in our lives. If we have neglected anyone or anything, allow us to ask for forgiveness and do better moving forward. Allow us to not be so overwhelmed with having a child that we forget to live the life that you have blessed us with. You are an amazing God, you do amazing things, and even though we don't always acknowledge you, we are grateful that you have never left our side even in times when you have to carry us.

We Love You. We Adore you. We Trust You.

Yours Truly,
Stephanie

Today I am grateful for...

Personal Reflection from this prayer

The infertility journey is not one that I would willingly take, but you, like me, decided to be "all in" because our desire to have a family outweighed our fears. Please remember my dear sister reading this book, no matter what the outcome, it is important for you to know that you've done everything in your power to make your dreams come true.

I am not sure where you are on your IVF journey, but what I want you to know is that I am proud of you for stepping out in Faith. IVF does not make you a failure or inadequate, in fact it proves just how strong and courageous you really are. My Hope, Prayers, and Desire for you is to trust God even when you don't know what is coming next. That you will hold tight to the fact that God has a plan for your life. God loves you, and He has not forgotten about you.

Blessings Always,

Stephanie

I would love for you to share your experiences with me either through email contact@renewedpc.com or socialmedia using the hashtag #pywtivf and be sure to tag @renewedpc on instagram and @SDJRPC of facebook.

Testimonials

God laid it on my heart to reach out to other women going through the same journey as I through prayer. These testimonials are the reason for this book. 'This is the confidence we have in approaching God: that if we ask anything according to his will, he hears us.' John 5:14

Going through IVF is hard! It's physically taxing, emotionally draining and spiritually exhausting. There were days when I literally didn't know how I was going to make it, but I knew I wanted my miracle baby more than anything in this world. I joined an online IVF community for support and to feel like I wasn't alone. Stephanie stood out amongst the crowd. Her words of wisdom were powerful, and poetic, and provided a sense of peace that was beyond understanding. She was ever-present, always there to pray for someone who needed comforting and a virtual hug. It made such a difference in my own spiritual journey during this time - I felt hopeful and blessed and encouraged. It eased the daily pain that came with the territory of trying to conceive and experiencing difficulties. Eventually my dreams came true. God blessed with my miracle baby girl, but I have Stephanie to thank for getting me the point where I was spiritually ready and open to receive God's gift. I am forever grateful. As a result, we are not only sisters in the IVF world, but we are sisters in Christ and Love.

Adrienne - New Jersey

My journey with infertility started at 19 when I got

married. Never would I have thought that I would be looking for my monthly but I couldn't wait for "Aunt Flo" to come knowing that I needed a period to start my family. As I got older, starting asking questions, I was finally given a diagnosis of polycystic ovarian syndrome or PCOS. For years I was told, I'd never be able to have a baby but was finally afforded the opportunity to undergo in vitro fertilization. This is when I met the beautiful Stephanie Jeffreys. She definitely became a burst of sunlight. Going from "Stop trying, it'll happen" , "You're time is coming", "You're young, be patient ", to having someone pray for me. Her prayers became my daily motivation to make it through the day with my head high and heart open for whatever my day consisted of. The daily prayers made it ok for me to go to bed at night, not pregnant but gave me hope that tomorrow may be my day. I was reassured that going to bed with no baby in my uterus was not my fault and that it would be ok. Every morning, I reached for my phone to get my daily affirmation to get me through the day. My outlook on my infertility changed from it being a curse and feeling damaged or inadequate to providing a reminder that I am superior with or without child which built my self confidence and self worth. Mrs. Jeffreys' prayers kept me sane when I thought I was going to lose it and wanted to give up. I stayed positive and my day came. I gave birth to a beautiful baby girl, November 23rd, 2015.

Donnetta - North Carolina

Going through IVF was the hardest thing I have ever done. I knew God had a perfect plan but that didn't make any of it easier. During those few weeks, I came to a place in my faith that I had never been before...complete surrender. I had to tell myself every single day and confess it to God that no matter what, I would still love and trust Him. The IVF support group I found on Facebook is where Stephanie comes into my story. She was a member and going through the journey herself and each and every day she posted these prayers...prayers that just spoke to my heart and soul. On more than one occasion, I would be going to yet another doctor's appointment or having a "poor pitiful me" moment, and I would see her prayers for the group and I knew it was God speaking to me. Her prayers were such an encouragement and comfort during the most difficult time in my life. Even though we have never met in person, she holds a special place in my heart for helping me through that journey.

Amanda - Georgia